Allie Alligator

A Lesson in Loving Your Enemies

Larraine Gowans

Illustrated by:
Gabrielle Angeles and Krizza Baguhin

Trilogy Christian Publishers
A Wholly Owned Subsidiary of Trinity Broadcasting Network
2442 Michelle Drive
Tustin, CA 92780

Copyright © 2022 by Larraine Gowans

All Scripture quotations, unless otherwise noted, taken from THE HOLY BIBLE, NEW INTERNATIONAL VERSION®, NIV® Copyright © 1973, 1978, 1984, 2011 by Biblica, Inc.® Used by permission. All rights reserved worldwide.

Scripture quotations marked (KJV) taken from *The Holy Bible, King James Version.* Cambridge Edition: 1769.

All rights reserved, including the right to reproduce this book or portions thereof in any form whatsoever.

Cover design by: Cornerstone Creative Solutions

For information, address Trilogy Christian Publishing
Rights Department, 2442 Michelle Drive, Tustin, Ca 92780.
Trilogy Christian Publishing/ TBN and colophon are trademarks of Trinity Broadcasting Network.

For information about special discounts for bulk purchases, please contact Trilogy Christian Publishing.

Manufactured in the United States of America

Trilogy Disclaimer: The views and content expressed in this book are those of the author and may not necessarily reflect the views and doctrine of Trilogy Christian Publishing or the Trinity Broadcasting Network.

10 9 8 7 6 5 4 3 2 1

Library of Congress Cataloging-in-Publication Data is available.

ISBN 978-1-68556-601-2
ISBN 978-1-68556-602-9 (ebook)

Dedicated to God, for giving me the inspiration to write this work. To my mother, who always believed in me, helped me, and encouraged me to follow my dreams. Also, to my husband and my three wonderful children, who are all my huge support system. I love you all.

Luke 6:27–36 (NKJV)

Love Your Enemies

27 But I say to you who hear: Love your enemies, do good to those who hate you, **28** bless those who curse you, and pray for those who spitefully use you. **29** To him who strikes you on the one cheek, offer the other also. And from him who takes away your cloak, do not withhold your tunic either. **30** Give to everyone who asks of you. And from him who takes away your goods do not ask them back. **31** And just as you want men to do to you, you also do to them likewise.

32 But if you love those who love you, what credit is that to you? For even sinners love those who love them. **33** And if you do good to those who do good to you, what credit is that to you? For even sinners do the same. **34** And if you lend to those from whom you hope to receive back, what credit is that to you? For even sinners lend to sinners to receive as much back. **35** But love your enemies, do good, and lend, hoping for nothing in return; and your reward will be great, and you will be sons of the Most High. For He is kind to the unthankful and evil. **36** Therefore be merciful, just as your Father also is merciful.

Once upon a time, in the freshwater marshes of Mississippi, lived an alligator named Allie. Allie had always been the biggest of the bunch, no matter where she went. Another big thing about Allie was her heart. She was always kind to others, no matter who they were or what their size.

Allie had all sorts of friends who lived in the marsh: beavers, birds, frogs, and fish, just to name a few. However, Allie's best friend was a cricket named Winifred. You wouldn't think that they would have a lot in common, especially because Allie was an alligator, and Winifred was a cricket. To tell you the truth, they didn't have much in common on the outside, but they had a lot in common on the inside.

This is a story about two friends who went through a great struggle together as they decided to share love with those who lived outside of their beloved marsh; more so, how they shared their love with one who most would say was their enemy.

They had met last summer, when Allie noticed what she thought was a very small leaf on a rock. As Allie moved to take a closer look, the leaf began to speak and explain that it was really a cricket. Winifred explained all about how crickets chirp, and that they can't swim.

Allie found Winifred fascinating and decided to tell her a little about alligators.

She explained that they love to swim, and have very big mouths that make grunting, snorting, and sometimes hissing sounds. She also told her how alligators come out of the water from time to time to get rest and soak up the sun. From that day on, the two began to talk every day about how they were different, and found out how much they were alike.

One hot summer day, Allie had just finished her morning swim when she heard a tiny voice from behind the tall green grass: "Hello, friend!" It was Winifred, Allie's longtime pal.

"How are you today, Winifred?" Allie asked, as she walked slowly out of the water.

"Well, I'm doing just wonderful. I wanted to know if you would like to join me on a walk through the grasses, close to the dryer land.

There are sure to be some of those messy mud puddles that you like!" said Winifred.

Allie smiled a bit but felt her stomach wiggling, which usually meant something was wrong. Allie looked at her cricket friend, who seemed so happy and excited to go to the dry land. Allie ignored the bad feeling that she got in her tummy and said, "Sure, I'll go with you—lead the way."

The way through the marsh to the dryer land was everything Winifred cricket had said it would be—*messy*—and Allie loved it! "This mud is great!" shouted Allie.

"I knew you would like it," said Winifred, as she bounded through the high grass, one blade at a time.

Sooner than they knew it, the marsh was coming to an end, and the dryer ground was in sight. Allie's tummy wiggled again. She ignored it a second time.

"Hey," said Winifred, "the dryer ground is right ahead. Care to sit in the sun with me for a bit, Allie?"

"Sure thing," agreed Allie. "I could use a break, and the nice, warm sun would do me some good too!"

Soon they were both lying in the sun, remembering all of the fun times they'd had together. They spoke about the pact they had made to always be there for one another and to treat all others with respect and love. Even if they were treated badly, they had decided they would show love, no matter what.

"That's a great pact that we made," Winifred said, "and I sure am glad we made it together." They both smiled as they looked up into the bright blue sky. They decided this would be the perfect spot for a nap!

They had started to drift off when they heard an unfamiliar sound, coming from a wooded area not too far away.

Whoosh...whoosh...

"What was that?" Winifred whispered.

"I don't know," Allie answered, in a low voice. By this time, Allie's stomach was wiggling out of control.

"Something's wrong," Allie stated. "My stomach has been wiggling ever since you asked me to come to the dryer ground."

Just then, they saw a big white boat being pushed out toward the marshy area. "Oh no, man is in the marshes!" Allie said with surprise.

"We must go back quickly to warn the others, before it's too late." Allie slowly moved toward the marsh. The mud covering her body allowed her to blend into the surroundings and hid her from the men. As soon as she was fully in the water, she was careful to keep low and began to swim as fast as she could, with Winifred leaping on the blades of grass beside her.

"What do you think they want?" Winifred asked.

"Well, man, also known as hunters, have been said to come around these parts to take alligators and other wildlife and fish away! I heard that once they take you away, you never come back again," Allie explained.

They soon arrived at the marsh area, where Allie's friend Daisy Alligator lived. "Daisy... Daisy!" cried Allie. "Man is on his way here, and they have a big white boat!"

Daisy came out of her burrow. "Quick, help me warn the others!" Daisy shouted.

Allie, Winifred, and Daisy warned all the alligators, wildlife friends, and fish about the hunters nearby. Everyone hid and made sure to stay away when they heard the white boat passing by. Everyone was safe...this time.

Later that night, Allie was awakened from her sleep by the sounds of clanging, banging, and pounding of running feet. Soon she heard human voices yelling, "We got another one! They surely do come out at night!"

Soon there was more clanging and bumping, followed by a boat motor starting. "This should be enough," said another hunter.

"Enough what?" Allie whispered to herself, as she hid in her underground burrow. Sounds of the boat slowly moving away sent Allie coming out of hiding to see what was going on. "Winifred? Daisy? Can you both hear me?"

Allie listened. "*Creek, creek... Chirp, chirp...*" Winifred jumped over to where her friend Allie was.

"Allie, we've got to do something—the hunters...they took five alligators, four beavers, and a bucket-load of fish!"

"Come on, let's go," grunted Allie. "I know just what to do."

Winifred wasn't sure of the plan but trusted her friend, so she followed closely behind, leaping quickly to keep up.

Soon they arrived at Allie's favorite aunt and uncle's burrow. "Allie," said a voice from behind a tree. It was Allie's Uncle Bob. "Thank goodness you're okay! The hunters...your parents...they're gone!"

Allie let out a loud hiss, followed by a loud *snap*! "*No*! Not Mama and Papa!"

Winifred looked down at the ground, sad with the news. "I'm sorry to hear that, Allie— what should we do? What can we do?"

"We will go to war!" cried Allie's Uncle Bob. "How dare they come into our homes and take away our families and friends! We must show them that we are not afraid to fight!"

Allie and Winifred looked at one another. Allie felt very upset that her parents had been taken away and asked, "What's the plan?"

"Well," said Uncle Bob, "you're a very large gator, Allie, and there are plenty of animals around our parts who would be terribly afraid to fight with you. I think you should lead us.

When they see your large body and huge jaws, followed by all of us here in the marsh, they will be sure to run."

Aunt Melinda jumped in and added, "Let's gather as many friends as possible and get moving as quickly as we can. I'm sure we can catch up to them."

The plan was off to a great start. They gathered as many friends as they could and started off toward the dryer ground, where Winifred and Allie had seen the white boat earlier that day. "I can smell them!" bellowed Allie. "We're almost there!"

Just then, Allie heard a noise coming from her right side as she swam toward the end of the marsh. She then saw the back end of the white boat. Hunters began to emerge from the boat, bringing tied-up gators and small cages and bins with the other wildlife.

"There they are!" creaked Winifred. "They are taking your parents out of that boat!" As the last hunter stepped out of the boat, he and the others began to push the boat toward the wooded area.

"Allie, move quick!" hissed her uncle. Allie swam as fast as she could, with her family and friends following closely behind.

The hunters turned around and saw Allie approaching. With great big *screech*es, the hunters began to take off, running and yelling.

"Quick, Jim," yelled one of them, "grab the gun—there's a big one coming right for you!" It was Allie, headed right toward the last hunter who jumped out of the boat.

The hunter tripped and fell, his leg stuck between a huge branch wedged in the mud.

"*Groooooaaar,*" bellowed Allie, quickly approaching the man.

"No, stop, I'm sorry, please don't hurt me... I didn't mean to..." Just then, Allie opened her mouth and hissed loudly. The man began to shake wildly, his foot still caught in the branch.

Allie looked at the man as she got closer. He tried to loosen his foot from the branch, but it wasn't working. He covered his face... Allie opened her jaws...and right before she closed down, a familiar voice yelled, *"Remember the pact!"*

Allie turned her head and saw Winifred leaping toward her, yelling, "Don't do it, Allie! No matter how big you are, be kind to others—even your enemies!"

"Not now," Allie grunted. She opened her jaws again, her body right in front of the hunter, looking at his body shaking wildly, and...*snap*! All was silent. The other hunters had fled away, and the animals of the marsh had their attention set on Allie. Allie emerged from the ground, turned toward Winifred, and released the large tree branch that had been wedged in the dirt from her mouth.

Allie began to move back slowly. Winifred leaped a little closer and saw…the hunter still on the ground, covering himself. He slowly lowered his arms from his face and looked for Allie.

Allie, who had backed away from the man, stood looking at him—then she noticed her parents lying on the ground a few feet away. She walked over to them and began to hit the ropes they were tied up in with her snout. She grunted, lowly. The hunter watched. He then began to look at the other animals, who walked closer to Allie.

He rose slowly from the ground, noticing that Allie had released his foot from the branch and spared his life. The hunter began to back away toward the wooded area, with a close eye on the marsh animals.

Allie bumped her nose on the ropes a second time and let out a pitiful, low, longer grunt. This time she lay her body flat to the ground and stared at them.

Her parents let out low grunts as they glanced in her direction. The other animals looked at Allie's parents sadly when they saw that their bodies were tied with rope and their mouths were taped shut. The hunter watched as he backed away and thought he understood.

He noticed a long hunting knife that one of the others must have dropped on his way out. He bent down slowly, picking up the knife, holding it close to the side of his leg. The marsh animals began to back toward the marsh when they saw the knife in his hand.

Allie raised herself from the ground and moved back a little as she noticed the hunter walking toward her parents. She then noticed one of the hunter's arms rising slightly in the air as he said, "Easy there, gator, easy…" sweat pouring from his brow. "I'm gonna cut them loose, because of what you've done for me." He slowly approached the back of Allie's mom and dad.

Winifred cricket could hardly breathe, as she was so nervous for Allie's parents. The hunter moved the knife slowly toward the back ropes of the gators while he held the other hand in the air as a sign of peace. "Allie," Winifred chirped, "move back a little more. I think he's trying to help your parents."

Allie moved back a little more, keeping a close eye on the hunter and his sharp knife. With that, the hunter used swift, small movements to cut the ropes from the alligators and saved their mouths, which were taped, for last. He then, very carefully, trying to keep as much distance as possible, released the tape from their mouths and ran off into the wooded area.

Allie's parents rushed to her and without hesitation, they all moved to the freshwater. The whole pack of animals swam back toward their home in the marsh. Winifred, leaping next to her best friend, said, "Allie, I'm very proud of you. You kept the pact, and for that, your parents were saved."

Allie smiled as she looked at her parents swimming, and said to herself, "I loved my enemy."

The next day, the animals that were taken from the marsh re-appeared! "They let us go," blubbed a fish. "This has never happened before," she said, as she swam happily away.

A few months later, as Allie and Winifred went for a swim and a friendly hop around the marshes, they saw signs posted around their marshes.

They then noticed a familiar figure posting a sign in the distance...it was the hunter who had freed Allie's parents! After the man finished placing his sign, he looked at the marshes, took a deep breath, and walked away. Allie and Winifred walked over to the sign. It read: NO HUNTING. MARSH PRESERVES.

"What does it mean?" asked Winifred.

Allie smiled, "It means that because we chose to love our enemies, our families will now be safe, forever." The two continued their walk and had nothing but smiles for the rest of the day.

Afterword

Luke 6:26 urges us to love our enemies and treat them as we would want to be treated. God said that if we only love those who love us, what reward would we get from this? As we see here, because of Allie's willingness to love her enemy even though he tried to hurt her, a great reward was given. Not only were her parents saved, but all of the animals in the marsh were saved from the hunters because of her one act of kindness. The hunter saw the compassion Allie showed when she snapped his foot loose from the wedged stick in the mud. He then decided to free her parents, and eventually helped post signs around Allie's marshes so that no one would be able to hurt any of the wildlife again.

Our actions make a difference. Whether we choose to love or disregard love makes a difference too. Just like Allie made a difference, one person can make a difference. *You* can make a difference! The next time someone mistreats you, show them love, pray for them, and see the wonderful ways God will move into the other person's heart and life. If you do not think that you are strong enough to love an enemy, pray that God will help to strengthen your heart, believe it, and He will help you to receive that kind of love! See how God will bless you and others around you! Continue in love! You can never go wrong.

1 Corinthians 13:13 (NIV)

And now these three remain: faith, hope, and love. But the greatest of these is love.

CPSIA information can be obtained
at www.ICGtesting.com
Printed in the USA
BVHW022256181122
652278BV00027B/2506